JIM HENSON

A Little Golden Book® Biography

Written and illustrated by Luke Flowers

A GOLDEN BOOK • NEW YORK

Golden Books
An imprint of Random House Children's Books
A division of Penguin Random House LLC
1745 Broadway, New York, NY 10019
penguinrandomhouse.com
rhcbooks.com

Library of Congress Control Number: 2024953000
ISBN 979-8-217-11855-7 (trade) — ISBN 979-8-217-11856-4 (ebook)
Manufactured in the United States of America
10 9 8 7 6 5 4 3 2 1
EU Contact: Penguin Random House Ireland, 32 Nassau Street, Dublin D02 YH68.
https://eu-contact.penguin.ie

USDA
EDGAR BERGAN & CHARLEY McCARTHY FLYING HATS
A CAN FULL OF FUN

James Maury Henson was born on September 24, 1936, in Greenville, Mississippi. Jim and his older brother grew up in a home filled with laughter and art.

Jim's grandmother made quilts, paintings, and crafts. She encouraged Jim to be creative. His dad was a wonderful storyteller. Jim loved hearing his stories as well as others on radio shows and in movies.

The Henson family moved to Maryland when Jim was in the fifth grade. Soon, they bought their first TV. Television was a new form of storytelling then, and Jim was fascinated by it! He loved watching variety shows featuring all kinds of performers. The programs with playful puppets were his favorite. He decided he wanted to work in television.

That dream came true when Jim was a senior in high school. A local TV station was looking for young puppeteers for a children's show. Jim built his first puppet, Pierre the Rat, and auditioned for the job. He got it!

The show only lasted a few weeks, but it was long enough for a director from another TV station to notice Jim's talent. He was hired to work on more shows as a puppeteer and a set builder.

In 1954, Jim was a freshman at the University of Maryland and had his own TV puppet series! *Sam and Friends* was a five-minute-long show that aired twice every weeknight. Working alongside him was a new friend named Jane Nebel. The two of them met at a college puppetry class. They made a great team.

Jim and Jane built more than a dozen puppets for the show. Jim came up with the idea to watch his performance on a monitor as they filmed the show. Seeing exactly what the TV audience would see helped him know where his puppets needed to be.

Jim used all sorts of materials to make his puppets. They were unique and fun, so he started calling them by a fun name. Instead of *puppets*, his creations were *Muppets*.

One of Jim's favorite Muppets to perform was Kermit. He made the hand puppet from his mother's old felt coat and half a Ping-Pong ball for each eye. From those simple materials, a star was born!

Soon Jim was asked to make commercials. He created two new puppet characters, Wilkins and Wontkins. They starred in more than one hundred ads for Wilkins Coffee. Jim's wacky sense of humor and ability to tell a story in just ten seconds made the commercials very popular.

On May 28, 1959, Jim and Jane got married. They bought a house in Bethesda, Maryland, and used the lower level as a Muppet-making workshop. The following year, Jim graduated from college and the first of their five children was born.

Their Muppet family was also starting to grow. Jim hired their first full-time employee to help them meet the demand for more Muppets.

Audiences fell in love with Jim's talk show appearances, thanks to the funny songs his Muppets sang. Jim traveled to New York so much for work, he decided to move his family there in 1963. That same year, their son Brian was born. The Muppets family also added new members to help design, build, and perform puppets with Jim.

When the Children's Television Workshop wanted to develop a new show for kids called *Sesame Street*, they knew Jim was perfect for the job. He created a neighborhood full of colorful characters. The most impressive was Big Bird—an eight-foot-tall, full-body puppet. Jim enjoyed performing best friends Bert and Ernie with his real-life friend Frank Oz.

Sesame Street went on the air on November 10, 1969, and the show continues to bring sunny days to kids all around the world.

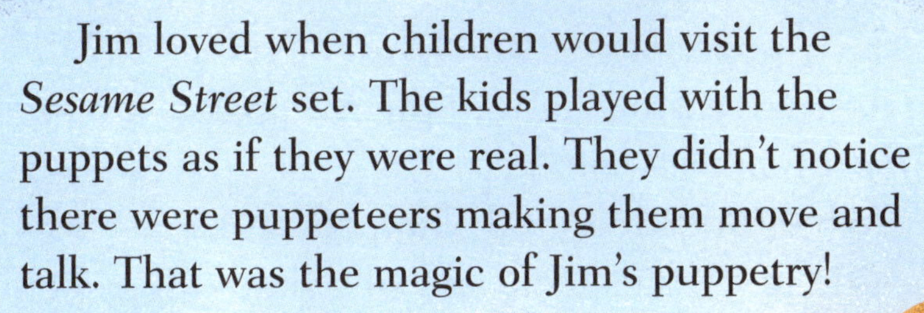

Jim loved when children would visit the *Sesame Street* set. The kids played with the puppets as if they were real. They didn't notice there were puppeteers making them move and talk. That was the magic of Jim's puppetry!

The Muppet Show, which premiered in 1976 and ran for five seasons, proved the Muppets were for people of all ages, not just little kids.

Each episode featured Muppets and a celebrity guest doing musical acts and silly skits—just like the variety shows Jim watched when he was young.

At the center of the chaos was the show's host, Kermit the Frog. Fozzie Bear, Miss Piggy, Gonzo, and the grumpy audience members Statler and Waldorf quickly became fan favorites.

The Muppets were a hit on TV. Soon, they would also become movie stars!

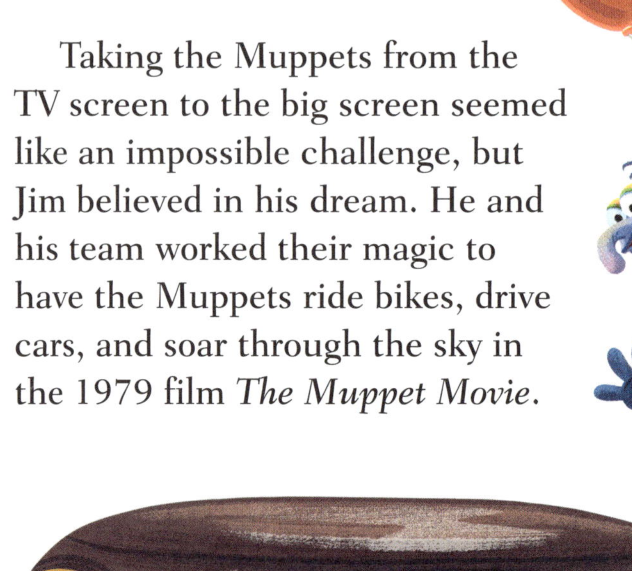

Taking the Muppets from the TV screen to the big screen seemed like an impossible challenge, but Jim believed in his dream. He and his team worked their magic to have the Muppets ride bikes, drive cars, and soar through the sky in the 1979 film *The Muppet Movie*.

It wasn't easy—to show Kermit singing "Rainbow Connection," Jim had to squeeze into a tank hidden underwater—but it was worth it! Audiences of all ages loved the movie. Kermit and the gang would go on to star in many more films.

When Jim's children were young, they often joined him on the set of his shows and films. By 1980, they were working alongside their father as assistants, puppet builders, and performers. Jim treasured these times with his talented family.

His teenage daughter Cheryl helped come up with the story for the 1982 movie *The Dark Crystal*. For this fantasy film, Jim didn't hire any actors. Instead, he and his team created a diverse cast of puppets—full-body puppets, hand puppets, and innovative new puppets that could move and change expressions by remote control. These animatronic puppets were built at Jim Henson's Creature Shop, where incredible puppets are still being made today.

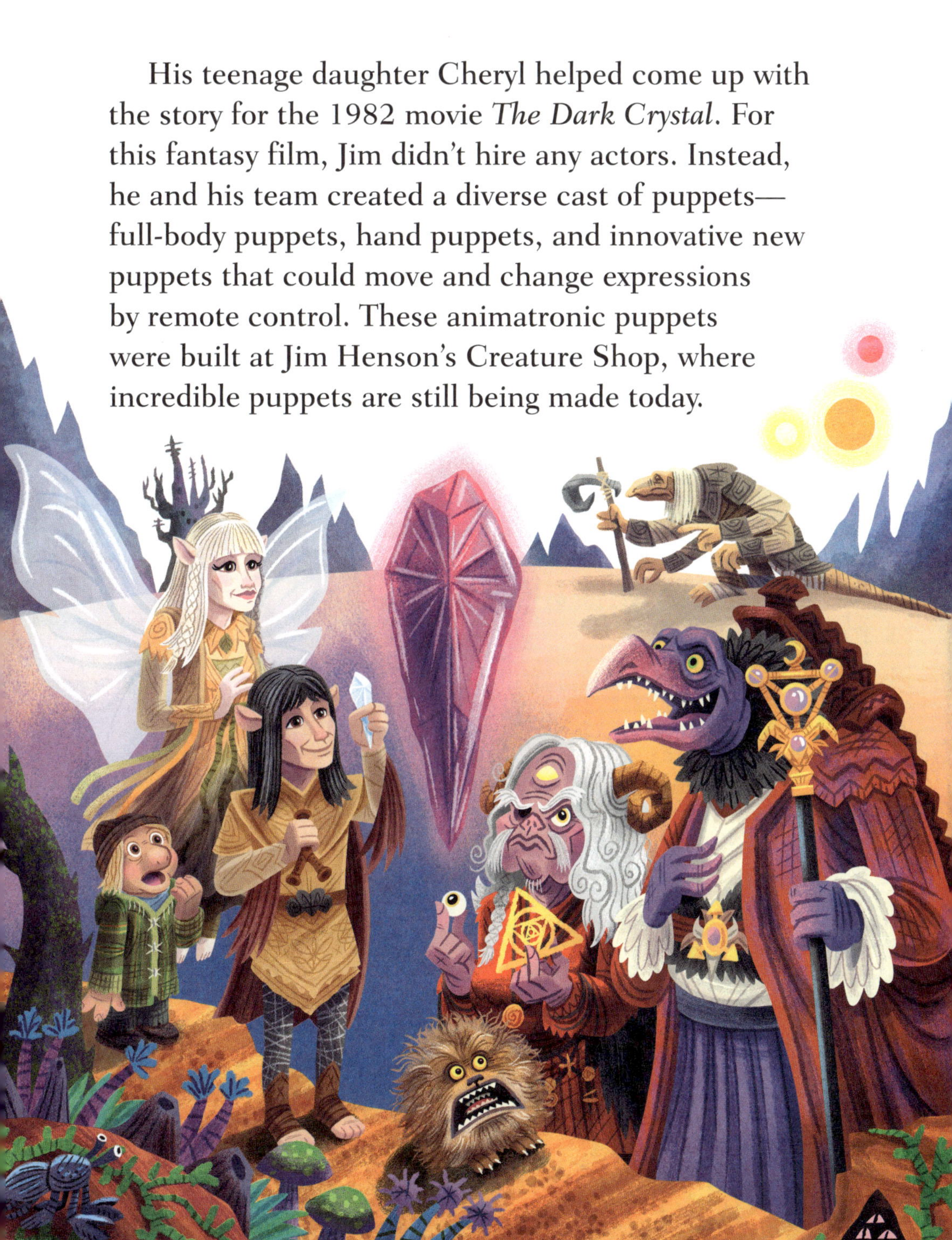

In 1983, Jim returned to children's television with a show called *Fraggle Rock*. It featured characters called Fraggles, who loved to dance their cares away, tiny hardworking Doozers, and giant Gorgs.

Jim hoped the program would teach children that all creatures can live together peacefully.

A scene in the film *The Muppets Take Manhattan* that shows several characters as babies inspired Jim to create an animated television show.

Muppet Babies featured young versions of Kermit and his friends having imaginative adventures in a nursery. The show kept kids smiling on Saturday mornings for eight seasons.

Working with other talented artists made Jim happy. He asked George Lucas to be the producer for his musical fantasy film *Labyrinth*. Jim had helped design the Yoda puppet for George's film *The Empire Strikes Back*. And Jim gave musician David Bowie the starring role as the Goblin King. Another multitalented artist on the team was Jim's son Brian. He voiced one of the main characters, Hoggle.

Jim's love of stories led to his television series *The Storyteller*. The award-winning show featured humans and puppets retelling classic folktales and legends. Once again, Brian Henson voiced several characters, including the Storyteller's dog. Brian was always inspired by his father's storytelling, just as Jim had admired his own father's stories.

Jim Henson passed away on May 16, 1990. He always said he wanted to leave the world a better place, and he certainly did. His imagination forever changed the art of puppetry. His characters have inspired people of all ages to create, believe, and dream. And his children, who continue to run their father's company, have ensured that the magic of Jim Henson will always bring happiness to the world.